As You and the Abused Person Journey Together

Sharon E. Cheston

Paulist Press
New York/Mahwah, New Jersey

Cover/book design and interior illustrations by Nicholas T. Markell.

Library of Congress Cataloging-in-Publication Data

Cheston, Sharon E.
    As you and the abused person journey together / Sharon E.
Cheston.
        p.   cm. — (IlluminationBooks)
    Includes bibliographical references (p.   ).
    ISBN 0-8091-3513-2
    1. Adult child sexual abuse victims—Rehabilitation.   2. Adult child
sexual abuse victims—Family relationships.   3. Child sexual abuse—
Psychological aspects.   4. Child sexual abuse—Religious aspects—
Christianity.   I. Title.   II. Series.
HV6570.C54   1994   94-30804
362.7′64—dc20   CIP

Published by Paulist Press
997 Macarthur Boulevard
Mahwah, New Jersey 07430

Printed and bound in the
United States of America

Contents

IlluminationBooks: A Foreword   v

Chapter One   1
    Introduction: A Friend in Need
Chapter Two   15
    What Are We Really Talking About?
    Definitions, Incidence, and Current Trends
Chapter Three   26
    The Support of Family and
    Friends Is Essential
Chapter Four   38
    The Course of Treatment
    (Or, What Goes On in the
    Therapist's Office?)
Chapter Five   51
    The End of Therapy/
    The Beginning of Thriving

Chapter Six   57
    Readying Yourself To Be of Help To
    Someone Who Has Experienced Childhood
    Sexual Abuse

Bibliography   62

Suggested Readings   63

IlluminationBooks
A Foreword

*I*lluminationBooks *bring to light wonder-ful ideas, helpful information, and sound spirituality in concise, illustra-tive, readable, and eminently practical works on topics of current concern. Learning from stress; interior peace; personal prayer; biblical aware-ness; walking with others in darkness; appreciat-ing the love already in our lives; spiritual discernment; uncovering helpful psychological antidotes for our tendency to worry too much at times; and important guides to improving inter-personal relations are only several of the areas which will be covered in this series.*

The goal of each IlluminationBook then is to provide great ideas, helpful steps, and needed inspiration in small volumes. Each book offers a new beginning for the reader to explore possibilities and embrace practicalities which can be employed in everyday life.

In today's busy and anxious world, Illumination-Books are meant to provide a source of support—without requiring an inordinate amount of time or prior preparation. Each small work stands on its own. Hopefully, the information provided not only will be nourishing in itself but also will encourage further exploration in the area.

One is obviously never done learning. With every morsel of wisdom each of these books provides, the goal is to keep the process of seeking knowledge ongoing even during busy times when sitting down with a larger work is impossible or undesirable.

However, more than information (as valuable as it is), at the base of each work in the series is a deep sense of *hope* that is based on a belief in the beautiful statement made by Jesus to his disciples and in turn to us: "You are my friends." (Jn 15:15)

As "friends of God" we must seek the presence of the Lord in ourselves, in others, in silence and solitude, in nature, and in daily situations. IlluminationBooks are designed to provide implicit and explicit opportunities to appreciate this reality in new ways. So, it is in this Spirit that this book and the other ones in the series are offered to you.

Robert J. Wicks
General Editor, IlluminationBooks

Chapter One

Introduction: A Friend in Need

*J*essica had spent the first half of her adult life meeting the expectations of society. She was educated, employed, married, and had 3 children. She greeted each day at dawn with a list of 20 things that had to be done by the end of that day. In this way, Jessica ran from early morning to late at night trying to meet everyone's needs.

On her oldest daughter's 8th birthday, Jessica awoke in a state of confusion. She had slowly been feeling overwhelmed by her life and all of its demands. She felt that her world was coming apart but she couldn't point to any one major thing that was wrong. Physically she felt tired and had no more energy in the morning than she did in the evening. She thought that she was coming down with a viral infection but she never developed any other symptoms. Jess frequently felt like crying over the smallest incidents and then made jokes about PMS even though the crying occurred every week of the month. Her concentration at work had diminished and, worst of all, she had felt estranged from God. Jessica had always felt very close to God and prayed often during the day even if it were a small prayer of one sentence.

Her daughter's birthday was supposed to be the beginning of a busy but exciting day, but Jess awoke feeling afraid, withdrawn, depressed, and confused. Her husband tried to reach out to her but she recoiled at his touch. Nothing looked right, nothing felt right. These feelings had been coming on for a while but this morning Jess felt like a ton of bricks had fallen on her. When her best friend, Maggie, stopped by to help her with the party, Jess was less than enthusiastic about the assistance that her friend was offering so Maggie left feeling rejected and angry.

Jess remembered feeling this way a few times in the past, when she had sex for the first time at 17; when she said "yes" to her husband's marriage proposal; when she found out that she was pregnant with her first child, John; and now here was that feeling again. All those other times she believed that the feelings were due to life stressors and transitions but there was nothing significant about a child's birthday; she had thrown her children birthday parties over a dozen times before this one.

During those other significant life transition times, Jess had ridden the feelings out and the anxiety passed within a few weeks. In fact, she was so adept at staying busy and hiding her feelings that, except for a couple of people who were very close to her, no one ever knew that anything was wrong with Jess. Co-workers and friends thought of her as competent but intense. She out-performed everyone and worked many more hours than others. However, they liked Jessica and knew that she was someone they could count on to be there for them even if they didn't feel particularly close to her.

This time when the intense emotions descended upon her, the feelings were ten times worse and yet the triggering event was ten times less stressful. In the past Jess resisted engaging in mental health counseling. She felt that she should be able to handle her own problems and she did not like the idea of paying for another person to "shrink her head." She had friends, her pastor, and family around her so she reasoned that they should be enough to get her through the pain this time, too. She reasoned that a stranger could not possibly understand her, that talking cannot change feeling, that counselors would see her faith as a crutch or something unhealthy, and that she didn't have the money. But this time she felt so out of control that she went to see her pastor, Kevin Nelson. He listened as she poured out her feelings which seemed to connect to nothing in her life. She wanted him to tell her that a pill, a prayer, or a vacation was all that she needed. He did not. He took her story very seriously and he told her that he was not equipped to handle her problem, and further, neither was she. Jess panicked. "My God," she thought, "I *am* really crazy." Sensing her terror, her pastor told her that she was not crazy, that he had heard many people describe similar feelings and that she needed a professional mental health counselor. He gave her two names and asked that she promise to call for initial interviews. Jess promised but then let 10 days go by hoping to handle this crisis herself but, after a week and a half, she did not feel better. Finally, because of the fear of needing professional help, Jess minimized the feelings of panic reasoning that all she needed was a good cry with her best friend, Maggie. She tried to garner an attitude of cheerfulness and invited Maggie for tea but when Maggie arrived she knew that something was still wrong. Maggie began to hypothesize about what had happened to Jess, coming up with a dozen ideas including Jess' marriage, her parents' health, her own health, problems with the children, etc. Maggie tried to engage Jess and then listen but Jess seemed distant and avoided speaking about the problem. Maggie attempted to cheer Jessica up but Jess seemed too preoccupied to notice Maggie's attempt at humor. Maggie was at a loss. First, Jess rejected her help on her daughter's birthday and now she felt that no matter how she approached her friend, Maggie could not do anything right with Jessica. Maggie knew that she was treading on difficult, uneven ground. What should she do; confront, plead, cry, withdraw, yell, demand, be silent, leave?

Jess sensed Maggie's uncomfortable feelings and became irritated because she expected that a best friend should be able to figure out what to do for her. The conversation was not going well and an argument ensued over nothing that was memorable. Maggie ended the conversation by stating that if Jess wasn't going to tell her what was bothering her then she was leaving. As Maggie walked out the door, she stated angrily that Jess was acting crazy. Instantly, Maggie was sorry for what she had said carelessly but she was so frustrated that she didn't know what to do to get Jessica to share.

A similar conversation took place with Jessica's husband, Fred. He insisted that she "get it off her chest." Jess yelled back that she didn't *know* what was wrong. Fred retorted that she'd better see a shrink and took the children to see a movie to give Jess some time to think.

That night she sat in front of the fire blazing in the fireplace and wanted to stick her head in the fire to end the pain. At that moment Jess knew that she was losing control and she immediately called the counselors Pastor Nelson had given her and left messages for them to return her call.

The first counselor to call heard the quiet panic in Jess's voice and the desperate, fearful cry for help and agreed to meet her the next morning. Jess assured her prospective therapist that she would be all right until her appointment just a few hours away. After hanging up the phone, Jess noticed that she felt a little calmer now that the initial contact was made. She reasoned that she did not have to go back if she did not like this "Ann" person who was nice enough on the phone.

That night, Jessica's dreams were a repetition of flashes about her childhood but none of the dreams made sense. In fact, she had had these glimpses of the past when she was awake too and, at various times, they were quite intrusive, usually occurring when she heard significant songs on the radio or when she smelled specific odors. Jess awoke feeling confused, anxious, and determined to rid herself of whatever emotional ghosts were haunting her.

The ride to Ann's office was a blur and as Jessica walked up the sidewalk to the office from her car she felt herself going numb. The office was tastefully decorated and Ann had a warm, welcoming demeanor that helped Jess feel more at ease. However, Jess blurted out that she did not want to be there in Ann's office and that she had good friends and family who could listen and give her advice. Ann agreed: "Family and friends are extremely important and a therapist could never take their places in your life. But also significant people in your life are not trained to help you in the same way a counselor is. You need both in your life for different reasons." Jess thought of Maggie, Fred, and Pastor Nelson; how they had tried to help; and ended up frustrated and angry. She began to understand that she needed all these people in her life but in various roles. She wondered what they could have done differently to make her understand how badly she needed help. As she sat there responding to Ann's questions, emotions began to swell up from deep within. Jess felt that she would explode but only a few tears emerged. "I'm afraid," Jess said hesitantly. "I'm afraid that something happened to me as a child that was so horrible that I don't want to remember it. I have flashes, impressions, dreams, and emotions which I cannot fully understand or control. For years I have been successful in suppressing these occurrences, but, all of a sudden, I am out of control. I feel as if I want to unlock the door and look in but I'm afraid that whatever is behind the door will devour me. Can you help?

Ann smiled. "Tell me what you remember."

That inviting sentence was the beginning of an uncovering process that could be compared to the unraveling of a golf ball. First, the hard resistant cover has to be opened and peeled away to reveal a seemingly endless wrapping of rubber-type bands which wind around and around the ball. Each unraveling brings the person closer and closer to the well-protected and undisclosed core. Once the ball is completely unwrapped the innermost part of the ball is revealed, a small perfectly formed ball which golfers will tell you is the heart of the golf ball and is extremely important to the way the ball performs. The person in therapy dealing with childhood sexual abuse will also be unraveling the memories and emotions of the past to finally arrive at the essence of herself. She needs her family and friends to provide essential support. As the

story of Jess' abuse became known to Ann and to Jess, Jessica began to deal with herself in a different manner. Instead of swallowing her pain she began to face it. This process affected her close relationships and each person who was involved with Jess needed to understand her journey to recovery. The more she knew about her abuse and comprehended emotionally what had happened to her, the more she gained control and was able to initiate new skills in dealing with herself, the significant people in her life, and God. As you read, you will see how Jessica traveled this path of discovery and what her support persons experienced and contributed to the process of healing. While Jessica's story is uniquely hers, there are major elements or patterns which seem to be present to some extent in every abuse scenario. Maggie, Fred, and Pastor Nelson felt the need to know more about what Jess was discovering and working through so that they could be of help to her in their own ways. Through Jess' journey, they discovered that childhood sexual abuse is one of the most horrific ills of our world. There is a palpable evil in the actions of the adult perpetrators that leaves lasting impressions on the delicate forming person of the young abused child. The abuse breeds anger, self-hatred, depression, rage toward others, and mistrust of authority, including our highest authority figure, God.

The good news is that people can and do survive, and with proper mental health treatment and appropriate, consistent support from their significant others, survivors can and do become thrivers. The journey is painful but the promises in the pain make the trek worthwhile. By following Jess' journey we will learn about the nature of sexual abuse, its symptoms, the long term effects, the necessary survival reactions the victim has, the type of therapeutic interventions which are helpful, the most enabling and encouraging responses that family and friends can make, and the faith implications which can interfere or enhance the person's relationship with God.

Importance of talking about childhood sexual abuse:
Why we all should be concerned

How many times have we all been told that the future of this world resides in our children? On some level we believe this to be true but our actions and priorities do not always reflect this value. The world spends more money on military weapons than on education and support for its future citizens. As recently as 60 years ago, children (and women) were considered to be the property of the male head of the family and therefore could be treated as the parent (and spouse) wished (Lew, 1990). In some countries men even held the ultimate life and death decision over children, and sometimes their wives. This belief has been challenged and in many ways completely eliminated in modern cultures but the elements of this belief still linger because attitudes do not change quickly. Until recently children had few if any legal rights and were not recognized as contributing members of society. As women and minorities began to demand equal rights under the law, our culture began to become more inclusive and tolerant of differences. Many would argue that we still have a long way to go but looking back 60 years will reveal just how far we have come in less than one generation's lifetime.

Children are now beginning to emerge as the next group of people who are in need of the recognition of their right to be treated with dignity. When a child is used for the sexual pleasure of an adult then that child's human rights have been violated. More important to the future of this planet is that the child is taught that older people are permitted to take advantage of younger people, that bigger people have more rights than smaller people, that when they are adults abuse of the next generation is permissible, and that getting one's desires met is more important than considering another's rights not to be harmed. These messages have been passed on from one generation to another. Our jails are filled with convicted men and women who have committed heinous actions against others and the major common history that they share is that 90% of them were abused by the significant adults in their lives, the very adults who were supposed to be protecting and nurturing them. As a consumer of daily news stories, I'm sure that you are baffled by the number of notorious criminals who make headlines. We follow their destructive paths, watch with relief when they are arrested, and gain satisfaction as they are tried and sentenced to life in prison or death. If however, you read about the *person*, you will usually discover a horrible childhood filled with sexual and/or physical abuse that was tortuous to the child.

This is not to excuse their actions or to imply that they deserve less punishment. These are dangerous people and need to be removed from our society. However, we cannot continue to ignore the fact that abuse yields abuse and that if we want a different type of world then we need to stop looking to politicians to pass laws to change our society and begin looking at the way we are treating the next generation. As Eliza Doolittle says at the end of *My Fair Lady*, it is not how you behave but how you are treated that determines who you become. In order to sexually abuse a child, the perpetrator must dehumanize the child and treat the child as an object that is appropriate to manipulate and forced to do as the adult wishes. Once a person is dehumanized and abused then that person will begin to act as a non-human. As we will see in a following topic on symptoms and ramifications, the acting as a non-human can take the form of many deeds, feelings, attitudes, and thoughts.

As a therapist, I can attest to the fact that what goes around comes around or, put another way, abuse yields more abuse. Not only is there a high probability that an abused child will grow up and abuse other children or act out against society by abusing others, but also the abused child may grow up and continue to abuse herself/himself. If our world is going to have a chance to survive, then we need to produce a next generation who are respected, loved, and given the opportunity to succeed at relationships as well as loving themselves. Talking about sexual abuse brings the issues into the foreground and causes us to take a stance on how destructive it is to a child and to our society as a whole. In addition, if these horrid activities are going to stop, we as a society need to stop excusing the perpetrator from accountability. If a child is sexually abused at home, then the system works hard to protect all members of the family including the perpetrator and the focus can often be on getting the family help so that they can resume living together as a family. However, let the same adult person sexually abuse a neighbor's child and we talk about locking the perpetrator up and throwing away the key. An also interesting comment on the inconsistency in our society is the fact that when incest occurs we name it as sick, family dysfunction, or crossing of parental boundaries, but if the same person has sex with the child's friend, we call the action rape and consider it illegal. We must begin changing this perception if children are going to be protected from abuse. The same attitude exists with physical abuse too. Beat your own child with a belt and it is treated by the courts and social services much differently than if you were to beat a neighbor's child. In the second incident you would be arrested for assault and battery. In other words, our laws are more lenient if the perpetrator sexually or physically harms his/her own child than if he/she harms another's child.

The media is helping to dispel the inconsistent treatment of offenders and society's beliefs by presenting the public with information in the form of movies, talk shows, and news reports on this topic which has been hushed up for so many years. But we have to be sure that the true information is presented and not only the notorious and widely publicized cases. Many adults whom you meet every day at work, in your neighborhood, in your church, and, perhaps, even in your own family are victims of sexual abuse. They are just as important and are in just as much pain as the guests of Geraldo. Jess will never be a public figure and if you met her you would not see any telltale signs of the abuse of so many years ago but she is the mother of three children and she is raising the next generation of citizens. If she is not mentally healthy how will she be able to raise healthy children? How could you help her in the pursuit of mental health for herself, and for her children, for her marriage, for your friendship and for our world?

Chapter Two

What Are We Really Talking About?: Definitions, Incidence, and Current Trends

*B*efore exploring the life of Jessica and the topic of sexual abuse, we need to take a look at a few definitions. Child sexual abuse: "Sexual contact between a child and another person who has some form of authority over that child is sexual abuse.... The critical issue is that some form of sexual activity is imposed on a subordinate by one with whom such conduct is inappropriate because of age difference or family relationship" (Leehan, 1993). While you may feel that this definition seems very broad, most authors and researchers have ceased placing any qualifications on this important issue. For example, several years ago if sex occurred between a 16 year old girl and a 23 year old man, the act was not considered to be sexual abuse. Others may have frowned upon the activity and judged the girl as "loose" and the man a "cradle robber," or, worse, may have stated that he "got lucky," but the fact is most likely no charges would be brought against the man unless the girl stated that she was unwilling. Even in this case the man might not be tried for rape if there was no observable injury or other evidence of forced sex. Today, however, this same scenario would be considered to be sexual abuse. What has changed over the ensuing years is the acknowledgment of how much impact power has on relationships. This impact is particularly awesome when the power is unequal as it is between and adult and a child. When adults who were sexually abused as children talk about their experiences as victims of sexual abuse, they report that they felt totally powerless in the face of their abusers even if their abusers never threatened them. In other words, the fact that the abuser was an adult meant that the child felt unable to resist out of *fear* that he/she would be hurt, abandoned by the adult, unloved, or cause a crisis in the family which could result in being removed from the family and placed in foster care. Therefore all sexual abuse between adults and children is now considered to be abusive.

Sex can also occur between two children. Frequently I have listened to adults recount their stories of sexual experimentation with other children. All children explore their bodies and are curious about others' bodies, especially those of the opposite sex. However, this type of activity becomes abuse when, once again, there is an unequal distribution of power; then the uneven powers leads to viewing the sexual activity as coercive where one child forces another child to participate and that child feels unable to resist or tell an adult out of fear of retaliation. Children can also gang up on one of their peers, forcing a child into sexual activity, and then threaten the child if he/she is not cooperative and silent. Child sexual abuse becomes incest when the abuser and the abused child are related to each other.

Sexual abuse can involve many different types of harmful activities. Some of the activities are very clearly abusive where the abuser could be prosecuted for the occurrence. However, there are other types of incidents which are also abusive but are more difficult to define as such. These actions by the perpetrator are explained to the child and others as something which is necessary for the child but, in fact, are performed because the abuser gets satisfaction and sexual pleasure out of the activity. I call this type of sex abuse "covert sexual abuse" because the activity involves the abuser using power to obtain what he/she wants under the guise of what is necessary for the child. The activity is labeled abusive because the child's welfare is really not considered to be of prime importance.

Below are some of the overt and covert sexually abusive activities which children and adults have reported that they have been forced to perform. The list is by no means comprehensive.

—Being touched in sexual areas
—Being shown sexual movies
—Being forced to listen to sexual talk
—Being made to pose for sexual photos
—Being subjected to unnecessary medical treatments that involve sexual areas of the child's body
—Being forced to perform oral sex on an adult or other child
—Being raped or penetrated with objects
—Being fondled, kissed, or held in such a way as to make a child feel uncomfortable
—Being physically punished in a sexual manner such as being forced to disrobe to receive a beating
—Being ritualistically tortured in a sexual manner
—Being made to watch sexual acts or look at sexual parts of others' bodies
—Being bathed in an intrusive way
—Being ridiculed about his/her body especially concerning sexuality
—Being encouraged into sexual activities
—Being told that his/her worth as a person is only for sex
—Being forced into child prostitution or pornography (Cheston, 1993)
—Being called names that are sexually derogatory, for example, whore, slut

The terms used to describe the child/adult who has been abused are *victim* and *survivor*. Often the word "survivor" is used to denote an adult who is not being abused today but who was abused in the past (Lew, 1990). Victim is often used to refer to someone who is currently experiencing abuse. I believe that the word "survivor" is a euphemism that clouds our perception of the ongoing pain that results from the abuse. When the sexual abuse ceases, the agony continues for years and can affect all areas of the victim's life, psychologically, physically, spiritually, intellectually, and socially. As one of my clients stated, "I was a victim then and I am a victim now. Everything I do is colored by the fact that I was sexually abused" (Cheston, 1993). Most victims want to do more than survive: they want to thrive. So for the purposes of this book, we will use the word "victim" to refer to the person who was abused.

Abuser and *perpetrator* refer to the person who abused the victim. The words are interchangeable but often the word "perpetrator" is utilized when dealing with the legal system.

Feelings, attitudes, and behaviors of the adult who was abused as a child

Adults who were abused as children have several beliefs about themselves, others, and God which can interfere with their ability to be happy and live well. The primary belief is that there is inherently something wrong with them. They tend to view others as "better"

than they are: wiser, stronger, healthier. To compensate, they can become dependent on others, incompetent at tasks so that others must rescue them, or overachievers in an attempt to prove to themselves that they really are able and to hide from others that there is something wrong with them. Jessica falls in the last category. She is a well-educated, competent worker, wife, and mother who can astound others with her ability to accomplish a great deal. The problem is that Jessica does not believe that she is competent so she over-works to prove to herself that she is fine. The busy schedule also allows her to keep intrusive thoughts and emotions in abeyance. As you picture yourself journeying with her throughout her discovery and recovery, keep in mind how she disguises her pain.

Another trait of the abused victim is the tendency not to trust self, others, and God. You have already seen how Jessica did not trust the therapist, her own perception, and later you will hear more about her belief and lack of trust in God. Because the lack of trust stems from the betrayal of an authority figure, these victims also tend to have difficulty getting close to others. Intimacy equals threat to victims so they draw a circle around themselves restricting intimacy so that no one can get close enough to hurt them.

Jessica's response to Maggie's willingness to help was to create anger so that Maggie would feel pushed away and keep her distance from the sore spot in Jessica's personality. Abused persons act as if they have a broken bone in their souls. They put on an emotional cast to protect the brokenness against further attacks. This cast helps protect but also keeps the vulnerable feelings from being tapped by another or even their own memories. They are therefore protected but lonely even with friends and family around. I call this the insulation-isolation cycle. The person is needy for love, affection, caring, and closeness but fears these and so insulates himself/herself and then as a result isolates himself/herself against the very needs he/she wants fulfilled. As we discuss Jessica's story, you will see this cycle played out over and over again with her spouse, her friend, her therapist, her pastor, and her children. As the person who is accompanying the victim, your job becomes one of avoiding getting entrapped in the cycle and therefore ending up participating in enabling the person to distance from you too much. However, you do need to respect the fact that he/she needs space or he/she will panic. This is a tough job of balancing the need for intimacy with personal space and privacy.

Your friend, spouse, or other close person may react in ways that look inconsistent, baffling, not healthy, childish, or even crazy. The reason for this is her/his need for defense. As a child who was abused she/he learned how to cope with the pain in the ways of a child. Now those very survival actions do not work for her/him as an adult. Because the trauma was so severe, the coping style needs to be powerful. Therefore, many learn the gift of dissociation. God blessed us with this gift and many people have attested to its wonderful ability to remove the pain quickly. This coping mechanism is not just useful in sexual abuse but is also helpful in any major highly threatening tragedy. For example, one client revealed to me that his car stalled on a railroad track and he saw a train coming. He desperately tried to get his seatbelt off but, because of the terror he felt, his fingers wouldn't work well. Just before the train hit his car, he saw the accident from above his car. In other words, God's gift of dissociation allowed him to leave his body just before the moment of impact so that he would be spared the pain. When he awoke after several days in the hospital, he recounted his tale to others and was able to describe to the police exactly what happened after the train hit the car despite being unconscious. He described the arrival of the ambulance and watched from above as the rescuers used the jaws of life to remove his body from the wreckage.

Sexually abused children also have the ability to dissociate and "leave their bodies" to go to a safer place so that it feels as if the abuse happened to someone else. The most extreme case of dissociation is the creation of multiple personalities where the child escapes the abuse by creating a separate personality to endure the pain while he/she "goes away" during the abuse.

The resulting feelings of rage against the abuse can also create panic in the child especially if the abuse is her/his parent or a beloved friend or family member. In this case, the child feels murderous rage and may even fantasize or dream about how he/she would like to kill or mutilate the perpetrator. Since children are taught by adults that these feelings are inappropriate or sinful, the abused child begins to deny, separate himself/herself, or change the feelings into more acceptable feelings. This process of denying feelings is the bedrock of helping the child to:

1. distrust himself/herself (my feelings are bad)
2. distrust others (they tell me not to feel the way I feel)
3. minimize the abuse (he only did it when he/she was drunk so he couldn't help himself/herself)
4. distort reality (I know that he/she knows best so I must have done something wrong)
5. distrust adults (they are all wrong or hurtful and you can't trust what they say or do)
6. distrust God (*he* didn't save me from the abuser hurting me so God must love the abuser more than he loves me)

However, even if the child is successful in repressing or distorting feelings, this does not mean that the original feelings go away. Quite the contrary, these feelings mutate to become bodily symptoms. In other words, the feelings are still there but hidden from the persons's conscious. However, they are just as powerful.

Consequently, the adult reacts not as the typical hurt or enraged child at the abuse but as an adult who hates all authority figures, who uses sex to manipulate or exploit others, who becomes overly nice so no one will see the true feeling, who avoids people, who doesn't care and acts out against everyone in society, who drinks or takes drugs to avoid the pain, who denies having any feelings at all, who withdraws from people by hiding in a computer or cabin in the woods, or who may act child-like, afraid to grow up for fear of becoming an abuser.

Chapter Three
The Support of Family and Friends Is Essential

*L*et's return to the time when Maggie was invited by Jess to have tea. Maggie is aware that Jess is experiencing some problems and she is open to helping. However Maggie expects that Jessica will simply state where Maggie can help. This assumption may be correct for a healthy person experiencing troubles but when a person is struggling with the interior troubles that result from childhood abuse, then the conversation is fraught with undercurrents and hidden meaning. Maggie was unaware of this as she arrived at Jessica's home. The key to entering into a conversation with a person who seems to be asking for help but is not sure how to begin talking is to set a few general goals for the conversation.

1. Promise yourself that you will listen patiently even if the other person does not want to talk. Remember that the abused person does not easily trust or risk exposing the real self so patience and trust building is essential.

2. Allow plenty of time for the two of you to be together. The victim may feel abandoned or rejected if you must leave during the conversation.

3. Leave your prejudices and strong feelings outside. Rather, be open and sensitive without allowing yourself to feel defensive if your friend becomes angry or begins attacking you.

4. Know your limitations. Your intentions to help are wonderful but when you are dealing with problems such as Jessica's you need to incorporate referral for professional help in your goals.

With all this new information and clear goals for your actions, you can now enter Jessica's house through Maggie's eyes. Maggie greets Jessica with a hug and a kiss on her cheek, their normal greeting. Maggie is careful not to avoid this tradition, for Jess may feel rejected, and she is also careful not to hold on too tight or Jess may feel scared of the intimacy. Jess appears extremely strained, that is, her eyes look red, puffy, and tired; her mouth is drawn tight in a smile that doesn't quite work to make one know that she is happy. Maggie, sensing the strain and wondering what the problem is goes slow.

Maggie: You look like you need a friend. (Gently reflecting Jess' physical appearance)

Jessica: Yeah.

Maggie: You've had a rough time? (Softly probing feelings)

Jessica: Yeah, its been rough.

Maggie: I'm here if you want to talk. (Open invitation with no pressure intended)

Jessica: I do and I don't. I don't know if anything will help.

Maggie: You sure sound ambivalent or is it confused? (Reflecting Jess' feelings)

Jessica: A little of both. I don't know if I can explain it.

Maggie: Take your time. (Giving Jess space to decide what and how much to share)

Jessica: I feel as if my whole world is falling apart.

Maggie: How so? (Asking for clarification because she still has no clue as to what is wrong)

Jessica: I woke up a few days ago with a horrible feeling of being emotionally overwhelmed. I don't know what's wrong.

Maggie: Did anything happen to cause this feeling?

Jessica: That's the strange thing, no, nothing. It was Sara's 8th birthday but that's not what caused *this*.

Maggie: How have you been since then?

Jessica: Lousy, I can't shake it. It's as though I know something awful is going to happen.

Maggie: Kind of like a premonition? (Asking for clarification to be sure Maggie understands)

Jessica: Yeah.

Maggie: That sounds scary! (Identifying with the feeling) Do you have any idea of what this feeling involves?

Jessica: No.

Maggie: Have you talked to anyone about this?

Jessica: Yeah, I went to see Pastor Nelson.

Maggie: Could I ask what he said? (Looking for information without pressure.)

Jessica: (Laughing) Yeah, he thinks I'm crazy.

Maggie: He said that? (Trying to clarify, knowing that he probably did not say that at all)

Jessica: Well, not in those words but he told me to see a shrink and gave me two names.

Maggie: That doesn't sound as if he thinks you're crazy. That sounds as if he thought that you could sort this out better with a professional. (Gentle, caring clarification)

Jessica: (Morosely) What's the difference?

Maggie: Mental health professionals help people sort out their feelings.

Jessica: (Heating up a bit) So you think I'm crazy too.

Maggie: No, just confused about all this.

Jessica; Then why can't you help me sort this stuff out?

Maggie: Because I'm not trained to do that. Look, if your car broke down in your driveway, you'd probably call me and we'd both look under the hood and talk about it but I can't fix your car. I don't have the skills and neither do you. So now we are both looking at what you're feeling and neither one of us has a clue as to why this is happening. Let's call someone who knows how to help.

Jessica is silent. She is very silent. Maggie is getting a little antsy about the silence and she's not sure if she should say anything. She can hear the clock ticking and she's getting nervous. Maggie starts reminding herself to stay calm and quiet. In her crisis intervention workshop she was taught to honor the person's silence but it is getting very uncomfortable. Jessica sighs and a tear rolls down her cheek. Maggie loves her friend and fellow parishioner and she wants to grab Jessica and hug her and make things right by taking over, making Jessica call the respected pastoral counselor down the street, talk to Jessica's husband and make him understand, tell Jessica's kids to be good to their mom for a while, take the committee chair over so Jessica doesn't have to worry....

Jessica: Okay.
Maggie: (startled) What?
Jessica: Okay, I'll call.
Maggie: (Shocked but remaining calm outside) Great. Do you need any names? I have....
Jessica: No, I'll call the two people that Pastor Nelson gave me. Only ...
Maggie: What?
Jessica: If I do this, when I do this, will you still be my

friend and visit with me in between sessions? I
need a friend, I think I'm in for a rough ride.
That's why I'm so scared to start this counseling
thing.

Maggie: Sure. I'll walk with you. (Pause) Why don't you
call right now while I'm here.

Jessica: No, I have to go to pick up Sara at Brownies. I'll
call later.

Maggie: Promise?

Jessica: Promise.

Let us look at what Maggie did that created the
atmosphere of help. First, she didn't say "What's wrong?"
She only stated what she observed. Remember that Jessica
has trouble with trust, authority, and intimacy. Jess needed to feel trusting of Maggie, in that Maggie was not
telling her what to do or how to act or feel. Also, Jess
needed to feel free to talk or not to talk so that she could
decide how close to let Maggie get near her broken and
sore heart. Jessica tried a little intimacy with Maggie but
did not tell her everything she knew to be true. Second,
Maggie did not pressure Jessica into talking. She merely
opened the door and left it ajar in a welcoming manner.
Third, Maggie did not tell Jessica what to think, how to
feel, or how to act. She only reflected back what Jess said.
Fourth, when Maggie needed clarification she asked a simple straightforward question. Fifth, Maggie did not force
Jess to reveal her feelings but she did acknowledge Jess'
feelings. Sixth, when Maggie knew that Jess was stretching

the truth, as in the example of Pastor Nelson's referral, she did not confront Jess, she only reacted in disbelief and astonishment. Seventh, Maggie clarified the misperception that Jess had about counseling in a simple straightforward way. Finally, Maggie did not jump in and rescue Jess from her feelings when Jess was quiet. Nor did Maggie try to fix Jessica's life even though Maggie felt like doing so.

In addition, Maggie used the same type of listening skills that all helpers are taught. She sat with Jess, looked her in the eye without staring, nodded, and said, "Uhuh" to let Jess know that she was listening. All of these skills helped Maggie to minister to her friend without really finding out what was wrong with Jess. In other words, Maggie sat on her curiosity and did not push Jess to reveal more than she was able. The reward and benefit of this tactic came when Jess asked if Maggie would walk her through the pain.

Fred, the terrified, anxious spouse

While a best friend is afraid for her friend, feels frustrated, and wants to rescue her friend from the pain she is feeling, the best friend goes back to her own home and has a means for defocusing on the pain that she has listened to for an hour or so. A spouse is living with the sex abuse victim and is aware of the minute by minute symptoms of the pain. He sees her face after she cries, watches her hands shake, observes her forgetfulness, worries about the children, and confronts the uncertainty about the future. He is also daily dealing with his own feelings about what is happening to his wife and has difficulty separating himself from her torment. In addition, he frequently has no clue as to what his wife is experiencing and why. He wants to help but he is afraid that any one word may create a horrible fight or add to his wife's pain. In Fred's case, he wants to help but doesn't know how, he wants his wife to hurry up and get over whatever is bothering her but feels guilty because he feels this desire is placing his own wishes ahead of Jessica's needs, and he is terrified about what may be wrong. His imagination is running wild. Fred has lain awake at night wondering if his wife is having an affair, a nervous breakdown, or is seriously ill. He feels that every moment of his day when he is around his wife he is walking on eggshells. He has no idea what he should do so he has done nothing. Fred knows that Jess went to see their pastor but she said nothing when she came home and he was afraid to ask her about the conversation. He also saw Maggie leaving the house so he suspects that Jess has talked to Maggie, too. Fred is baffled as to why Jessica is not talking to him, for after all, he is her husband and they are supposed to love and trust each other. He cannot comprehend why she has felt the freedom to talk to two people outside the family when she is not sharing with him. The only conclusion that Fred can come to is that Jessica is having an affair or she has fallen out of love with him. Fred decides to go to see their pastor hoping that he can get some clarity.

Pastor Nelson was anxious about seeing Fred. He knew that he could not break Jessica's confidence by telling Fred what had transpired between them. He hoped that Jess had also confided in her husband. Within a minute of the beginning of the conversation, Pastor Nelson assessed that Fred knew nothing of Jess' struggle. What in heaven should he say? The pastor listened to Fred speak of the trials at home and his suspicion of an affair, his worry that Jess was ill, or having a nervous breakdown and knew that as a pastor who had heard Jessica's story in confidence he could say nothing to ease Fred's pain. Pastor Nelson felt totally stymied.

He listened to Fred pour out his heart through the tears of fear and panic and knew that he could help this man to gain some perspective but he had to honor the confidence. He felt anger at Jessica for keeping Fred in the dark when she could have eased his terror and gained some support for herself as well. When Fred was through speaking, he sat in the chair like a limp noodle feeling better that he shared his pain but emotionally exhausted. Pastor Nelson tried to assure Fred but knew that Fred was wanting more. Finally, he suggested that Fred talk to his wife but Fred rejected the idea, for after all, he reasoned, if Jess wanted to speak to him she would have done so. Pastor Nelson decided to give Fred some pointers as to how he could approach Jessica.

Fred listened as Pastor Nelson suggested that Fred find a large block of time when the children were not home and gently ask Jessica to explain what she was experiencing and feeling. Pastor Nelson told Fred to affirm his love to his wife and ask her to share what she was going through. Fred agreed even though he knew that he had asked Jessica several times to explain and she had repeatedly stated that she didn't know what was going on. Pastor Nelson insisted that Fred try again but that this time he suspend all of his needs and attend to his wife.

When Fred left the office, the pastor prayed that Jessica would share openly with the man who loved her so much. Fred prayed too; he prayed that he would find the right words when he talked to Jess.

Later that night Fred arranged for his mother to take the children for the evening so that he and Jess could have some time alone. Fred shook as he made one of their favorite dinners. Jessica was confused by Fred's behavior but felt calmed by the atmosphere he was creating. After dinner Fred used a moment of silence to broach the subject. He first told Jessica that he loved her and wanted to help her in any way that he could. He spoke slowly and quietly. Jess was receptive but quiet but she stopped looking Fred in his eyes. Fred thought that he had lost her attention. He knew that this conversation was going to end like all the others but he prayed that he would be able to re-engage Jessica. Fred took a deep breath. "Jessica, I love you and, no matter what, I want to try to understand and be with you as you struggle with whatever you are experiencing. Won't you please share with me what you do know even if it hurts me." Jessica looked at Fred in a puzzled manner. Fred tried again, "Jess, are you confused about us? Are you in love with someone else?" Jessica's eyes widened in disbelief. She never thought that her

behavior and silence was being interpreted in such a way. Jess began to shake her head vigorously and say "no." Fred was relieved as he felt the tears roll down his face. He grabbed Jess' hand and asked her to share what she felt. Jess poured out all that she had been thinking and feeling in the last two weeks. They sat that night and hugged as they cried and talked. Fred told Jess to see the therapist of her choice and that he would go too, if she needed him to be there. When Jessica walked into the office for her second session, she felt the support of her husband and her best friend. Somehow this affirmation gave her strength.

Chapter Four

The Course of Treatment (Or, What Goes On in the Therapist's Office?)

*E*ach therapeutic journey is unique but within each journey there are processes which are the same for each person. While we are only looking at one case, Jessica's story will generally parallel the trek toward health of other men and women.

Phase One: Engagement. Therapy begins with the first telephone call. The therapist's posture during that initial voice contact can make the difference in whether the client will show up or not. Ann demonstrated her excellent bonding capacity during that late evening phone call from Jessica. Sensing the need for immediate follow-through, Ann met Jessica the very next morning. Ann made the decision out of her knowledge that when a client finally decides to call, then a quick follow-up will more likely avoid a "no-show" because a person may back out if there is too much time between the appointment call and the first appointment (Cheston, 1991). Also, when a therapist can meet the client soon after the call is made, the client has the feeling that the therapist believes that he/she is important. Ann also checked out Jessica's suicidal ideas before she let Jess hang up the phone. The first session is an important meeting because the client is extremely anxious about entering therapy and usually is looking for an excuse to run away to avoid having to enter therapy.

Jessica saw Ann as warm and inviting. This made her feel more comfortable about talking to a stranger about her innermost feelings and thoughts. The first few sessions have several goals: 1) to become acquainted with each other, 2) to begin the process of bonding as a therapeutic team, 3) to hear the client's story, 4) to establish the therapy contract as to when to meet, how often, the fee and other housekeeping items, and 5) to allow the therapist to arrive at an initial tentative diagnosis of evaluation.

Jessica's experience with Ann was no exception to the above first stage processes. She was anxious and wanted to run away, she felt some initial trust in Ann but was still cautious, she used the first meeting to assess whether Ann could help her, and she believed that she could work with Ann because of Ann's early establishment of an atmosphere of trust. This is not to mean that the first sessions are emotionally easy. Jessica could feel

the power of her emotions rising to the surface as she was flooded with flashes of memory that she had had before. Ann was able to encourage Jess to share her story and the following is the background information that Ann heard in those few weeks.

Jessica is the first-born of three girls. Her younger sisters were born 2 years and 4 years after Jess. She grew up in an intact middle class family. Her father was a banker and her mother was responsible for the home and kids. Jess has felt that something was wrong with her ever since she was very little. She remembered that she hated it when her father would come home. He drank quite a bit on the weekends and would become nasty at times and overly affectionate at other times. Jessica's mother was ineffective in dealing with Jess' father. When he was out of control with his drinking or beating one of the girls, Jessica's mother stood by crying with the other two girls. Early on she learned that she could not count on her mother to protect her from her father's rage. Therefore, Jess learned to protect herself by becoming so busy that she was frequently out of the house especially as she became a teen and could find her own rides or drive herself.

Jessica's memories were spotty but highly detailed in several places. What bothered her more than anything were the flashes of memories that seemed unconnected to the other memories. She remembered seeing her naked father standing in her bedroom. Her strangest flash was of seeing a mirror that reflected the outside sky and clouds. Another flash was of her father sleeping in a bed but Jessica saw him from the upper corner of a room that she didn't recognize. The flash that bothered Jess the most was a simple kiss that her father gave her one day when she returned home from spending a week at a friend's house. The kiss was brief but her father had slightly parted his lips and she could feel his teeth as he kissed her. She also remembered his hugging her closely and picking Jess up so that her feet left the ground. In doing so her legs swung a little and she could feel her body being pressed into his groin. This "memory" confuses her because she does not remember this incident but just the feeling in her body and it made her sick to her stomach.

With all these feelings, self-image beliefs, flashing memories, and behaviors Jessica maneuvered herself through life maturing physically but feeling like a little girl inside. In fact, the very behaviors and self-talk that helped her survive as a child are the behaviors and self-talk that are keeping her from functioning at her best as an adult. Reviewing these at this moment will help us to see how the therapist is going to help Jess to psychologically mature so that she has reached the same level of maturity in both areas and, more importantly, we will be able to see how her family and significant friends can aid her in this important life transition in which she has chosen to engage.

1. Jess tells herself that there is something inherently wrong with her. For anyone to have degraded her by abusing her, there must be something awful about her that she deserved this treatment. Remember. this is the

way a child views her world, not the adult. In other words, this is the emotional state of a child, not the intellectual state of an adult.

2. Jess' feelings surrounding the abuse hurts her a great deal and at times the feelings overwhelm her as we observed on her daughter's 8th birthday. She discovered long ago that keeping very busy helps to hide the pain so she has a tendency to run from dawn to bedtime keeping very busy to keep the pain away.

3. Jess believes that she as a person is worth very little. She feels like "damaged goods" and therefore is not as good as others. Therefore, she serves others without taking care of herself because she does not feel that she deserves the care while others do. Her busy schedule insulates her from the pain and her insecurity isolates her from others.

4. Jess' relationship with God has been affected greatly but she acts as if there is nothing wrong. She is an excellent church worker, every pastor's dream. However, she works because she is convinced that she must work hard to earn her way to heaven since she is so poor a person that she cannot be loved by God just because she is Jessica. In other words, she is limiting God's love for her while she would refuse to accept God's love as limited when concerning her children, spouse, friends, and Sunday school students. But Jess does not believe that she was created as they were—out of God's love.

5. Jessica is hurt and angry with God the Father. She cannot figure out why she had to endure the degrad-

ing and hurtful actions of her father while everyone else has had wonderful childhood experiences. The only way that the little girl of Jessica can make sense of all this trauma is to say that God, the *Father*, must have condoned the action of her *father*. Therefore, God loves fathers more than he loves little girls, specifically, Jessica.

In other words, Jessica feels SHAME. Whereas guilt is a feeling about something that you *do*, shame is a feeling about who you are.

Phase Two: Working through the Abuse. Now it is time to do the hard work of therapy. Ann will ask Jess to participate in a number of difficult tasks which are intended to help Jessica to address the issues above. So far, Jess has the support of the people in her life, a willingness to work, and a strong therapist. Now the journey enters the difficult stretch of road. At times, she will want to quit, claim to be all better to avoid returning to her therapist's office, pick fights to make Ann reject her, and may look for signs of Ann's betrayal. Her significant others will have to be aware of these attempts to truncate the therapy when the pain becomes unbearable for Jess. Their presence and affirmation of her is going to be critical for her to stay in therapy. They are also going to have to have faith in the therapeutic process no matter how hard Jess tries to undermine her healing. Each person will make a unique contribution to this important phase.

Let's take a peek at a therapy session and see how the process is developing. Ann is sitting quietly asking

Jessica to consider a technique called empty chair. She is asking Jessica to put her traumatized child in another chair in the office and have a conversation with her child. At this time in therapy, approximately 3 months have gone by and Jess is getting quite resistant to Ann's suggestions. At the beginning, when they were working to uncover the memories, Jessica was compliant. She participated in the process and shared eagerly with her husband and Maggie what she was discovering in therapy. She was able to get in touch with her rage and look at the abuse, cry, get angry, and hate her father. In fact, Jessica told everyone what a wonderful therapist Ann is. She adored Ann and looked forward to seeing her each week. Jessica felt much better. Her symptoms that brought her into therapy were lessening. She felt less and less overwhelmed, she acknowledged that she needed help, and her mood was definitely elevated. The single greatest breakthrough, as far as Jess was concerned, was the realization that the severe sexual abuse had started just after her 8th birthday. When she realized that her daughter's birthday had triggered her emotional response 3 months before, Jess felt that she had the connecting link she needed.

Now, here is Ann asking Jess to talk to her make-believe child! Jess thought "How stupid!" Jess tries to do as Ann asks but she really feels self-conscious and Ann is not rescuing her from the dumb task. For the first time since she started therapy, Jess begins to think that she may have made a mistake in her selection of a therapist. Perhaps, Jess reasoned, Ann doesn't know what to do next. Maybe Ann is getting weird on her. Maybe Jess is all better and Ann just wants the money so she's making up the exercise to keep Jess engaged. Ann sits and waits for Jess to talk to her little child, Jessie. The session comes to an end and Jess avoided having to engage in this "dumb" exercise. She leaves the session feeling depressed and confused. Wasn't this the very reason she had first entered therapy? She felt as though she were back to square one. On her way home, she stops at the church hoping to catch Pastor Nelson. He only had a few minutes but he was glad to see Jessica. "I need the name of the other therapist you gave me six months ago. I threw it away after I started seeing Ann," Jessica explains. Pastor Nelson is in a hurry and it would be easier to give the name to Jess than to ask her to explain but he guessed that something was happening in therapy to cause Jess to want the name so he asks her to elaborate. Jess explains briefly what happened and why she needed the name. Pastor Nelson had guessed correctly. Instead of agreeing with Jess, he gently but firmly asks her to reconsider and to share her feelings with Ann. Jess was taken by surprise. She didn't want to share her feelings with Ann, she wanted to leave Ann. Pastor Nelson reminds her that running away does not help and further suggests that perhaps Jess wants to run away rather than confront the small hurt child who is the seat of all the shame and terror. Jess was furious but as always acted as a lady. She runs away (politely) from Pastor Nelson, figuring that Ann probably talked to him the minute Jess had left the office. For after all, don't all professionals stick together—probably even share kickbacks for referrals? Jess recognized how stupid she sounded but she was hurt and felt betrayed by the two helpers she counted on.

When she arrived home, Fred asked how therapy had gone as they prepared dinner together. "Wrong question!" Fred thought as Jess launched into her tirade. Her rage at Ann's therapeutic task poured out. Fred stood in the middle of the kitchen trying to follow Jessica's train of thought and wondering why she was overreacting and, further, wondering what he was going to say in response. Finally, his wife stopped her angry outburst and looked at Fred expectantly. Fred weighed all the various thoughts he had had while she had been speaking and he had no idea as to how to respond. Finally, Fred simply said, "Wow, are you angry!" Because Fred allowed Jessica to own her feelings, she did not become immediately hostile. As they talked Jess could sense Fred did not approve of her changing therapists. In fact, Fred hinted that Jess might want to try the exercise to see if it really helped. Jess sulked for the rest of the dinner and then announced that she was going to drive over and see Maggie. Fred fought the temptation to call Maggie and warn her; he felt that he would be placing himself in the middle if he did, so he busied himself with getting the children ready for bed and prayed for Maggie.

When her best friend opened the door, she could tell by the look on Jess' face that something was wrong. Asking Jess in and inquiring about her reason for dropping by yielded the same rage that she had unleashed on her husband earlier and her pastor that afternoon. Once again the recipient of the barrage of anger was stunned. Once again words were difficult to come by, so Maggie asked if Jessica had told her therapist how she felt. Jess responded than Ann would not understand and would insist that she was making it all up. Jess then volunteered that Pastor Nelson had told her to talk to Ann and that Fred had suggested that she try the exercise before she condemned the strategy. Jess further stated that they had probably both talked behind her back to Ann. Maggie took a deep breath and began slowly and carefully choosing her words. "Jess, you are my best friend and I love you, but you really need to look at a couple of things. First, Ann cannot talk to Pastor Nelson or Fred without your being present or without your permission, so it doesn't make sense that she would jeopardize her career to do so. Second, you put your trust in Ann and loved the way your therapy was progressing so why are you reacting so very strongly to a simple exercise?" Jess was stunned. Three times she had tried to get someone to agree with her viewpoint and three times the people had not supported her. She felt her depression clouding in around her as she left Maggie's house. When she arrived home she went to her bedroom, closed the door, and left a message on Ann's answering machine that she needed an extra session soon. Ann returned the call the next morning and scheduled an appointment.

After Jess explained what had happened after she left Ann's office, Ann asked a key question. "Why do you not want to talk to the abused child?" Jessica had not considered that her resistance to the empty chair technique was really resistance to seeing herself as the abused child. As the tears began to flow, Jessica quietly stated through clenched teeth that the child was worthless and weak. "Do you realize that you are talking about yourself?" asked Ann. Jessica nodded and dissolved into tears explaining how worthless she felt, how not only did her father abuse her but her mother refused to believe her, stating that she was a wicked child for having made up such a terrible lie. At the heart of Jessica's self-worth is the conviction that she was not worth believing or saving from harm. Her angry response to the request to try the empty chair scenario was basically due to her hatred of herself as a child and her second response was to see the three people she turned to as not believing her perception of her story about Ann, just as her mother used to do to her when she attempted to state her perception of her abusive father. The insight concerning the patterns of behavior was profound and then Jessica was able to see other times in her life where she had repeated the same pattern of thinking and reacting.

Then, as Jessica was considering her self-defeating pattern of thinking and responding, she had an insight about her relationship with God. Ann noticed something was going on behind Jess' eyes because her usual lively chatter had ceased and she had a glazed look in her eyes as if she were viewing her soul for the first time. She hated herself and yet God had created her in love. Could she trust God, the *Father*, and his view of her? If he loved her, why did he betray her and let awful things happen? Ann and Jess spent the next few months working together to change Jessica's unhealthy ways of thinking, feeling, behaving, and believing. She also recommended that Jessica spend some time in spiritual direction with Pastor Nelson. Jessica enjoyed her special time with her pastor, talking and praying about her feelings of betrayal by God as well as her belief that God didn't love her as much as her abusive father. Finally, she had to confront the issue of forgiveness of both her father and mother.

As the months went by Jessica found that she had worked through many of the issues which she had brought into therapy. She also recognized that she had more questions than answers but that pursuing the questions from here on could be fun, especially if she had a husband, best friend, and pastor on whom to bounce ideas.

Chapter Five
The End of Therapy/
The Beginning of Thriving

As Jessica began to feel, think, and behave in healthier ways, she began to worry about not seeing Ann in therapy anymore. She knew that she had a wonderful support system to help her in the future but Ann was a different type of support. Fred, Maggie, and Pastor Nelson had noticed the difference in Jess and complemented her on her hard work. These comments were constant reminders of the end of a relationship that had meant so much to Jess. She began to feel a little panicky and would remind everyone that she still had issues which needed attention. Then the day came when

Jessica sat in Ann's office as she had for so many sessions and couldn't think of any topics that needed addressing. Ann mentioned that perhaps it was time to think of reducing the number of sessions to once or twice a month. Jess smiled and nodded, but what was going on in her head was "There it is! I knew that she would reject me sooner or later." Jessica knew that the thought was irrational and part of the problem of her childhood patterns so she used the cognitive restructuring tool that she had learned from Ann and it worked. But this only made her feel worse because now she knew that she was ready to stop therapy.

The next weekend Jess and Fred held a party for several guests including Maggie and her husband and Pastor Nelson and his wife. As the time of the party neared, Jess became more and more agitated. Fred tried to calm her down but she only responded with a sarcastic statement. By the time the party began Fred and Jess were hardly civil to each other. Fred feared that Jessica had experienced a major setback in Ann's office a couple of days earlier. Jessica was out of control again. She was either accusing Fred of liking other women at the party, claiming that no one liked her, or criticizing her guests behind their back. Maggie was embarrassed, Pastor Nelson was confused, and Fred was angry. After the party Fred told Jess that her behavior was inexcusable and that she should not stop therapy no matter what Ann said. Fred concluded that Jess was not ready to be on her own and that perhaps Ann had misjudged Jess' progress because she was too close to see what was really going on with Jessica. The next day Fred threw caution and objectivity to the wind and called Ann to let her know what had happened. Fortunately, Ann was not in so Fred used up most of Ann's answering machine tape explaining what had happened and how he believed that therapy was ending too soon. Ann could not have talked to Jess' husband without Jessica's consent, so she was relieved that he had used her answering machine as a tool to vent his frustration.

Three days later, Ann saw Jess for what was supposed to be their final weekly session as they moved into a once a month schedule. Jess arrived with a faint smile on her face announcing to Ann that there had been a crisis over the weekend and that Fred said she should continue therapy. Ann only asked one question, "What happened!" Jessica related the story from her point of view and it was remarkably similar to Fred's frantic message on her machine. Jessica took all of the responsibility for the fight and for her behavior. She almost told of her inappropriate behavior with glee. Ann did not challenge Jess or probe for why she had acted the way she had. She merely stated, "I'll miss you too."

Jessica began to grieve as she had never before grieved in her life. She sat crying and rocking and a moan began to emerge from way down deep. She was at last grieving the loss of her childhood, the loss of her two parents who were supposed to take care of her and instead abused and rejected her, the loss of her dreams of having

a wonderful set of parents, and, of course, the ending of a relationship with the person who helped her grow up, Ann.

Ann gave Jess a couple of going-away suggestions to use until they saw each other in a month.

1. "When you feel stressed and need someone to care for you as your parents should have, seek out your husband or friend and enjoy his/her company."

2. "If you cannot be with them then soothe yourself. Buy a flower, listen to some of your favorite music, go to the perfume counter and try a new scent, savor your favorite cup of tea, or take a bubble bath." (Linehan, 1993)

3. "Imagine yourself in a secret room where you feel safe, and pray."

4. "Remove all of the high octane words (e.g. hate, rage, always, never) from your vocabulary to reduce the powerful feeling that is causing you stress."

5. "Turn your attention to an enjoyable activity."

Jess wrote down the suggestions and took them home. She couldn't wait to see Maggie, Fred, and Pastor Nelson. They had stood by her even when they did not understand what was occurring. They had loved her, supported her, listened to her, and disagreed with her when necessary. They were partly responsible for her growth, as was Ann. But the person who had done the yeoman's work was herself. She began to acknowledge that no one could make her change, she had to do that all by herself. She spied a florist on the way home and stopped and sent flowers to all four of them. She signed the card "I did it! But not without your support, love, and belief in me. Love, Jessica."

Chapter Six

Readying Yourself To Be of Help to Someone Who Has Experienced Childhood Sexual Abuse

*E*xperts and researchers in the field of counseling and psychotherapy estimate that one out of every 3-5 people has experienced sexual abuse in childhood. Their clinical practices are filled with men and women who are now seeking assistance for their shattered childhoods wherein they experienced trauma. Clinicians have found that as high as 70% of those seeking help were sexually abused as children (Briere and Runtz, 1991). What this means to you is that when you are sitting in a congregation worshiping with 100 people, approximately 20-30 of them were abused sexually as

children. You can help. God's instructions are clear to us.

Get rid of all bitterness, rage and anger, brawling and slander, along with every form of malice. Be kind and compassionate to one another, and forgiving each other, just as in Christ God forgave you. (Eph. 4:31-32)

As you minister to everyone you meet it will be difficult to discern when someone is reacting in negative ways because of the pain of child abuse or because of another reason. Your job then is to deliberately try to eliminate anger, slander or any malice so that the person is not further traumatized inadvertently by you. If we meet and treat others as we would want to be treated then we will be in the perfect place to act as a support system to someone who may seek us out for reassurance or assistance in connecting and maintaining a nurturing relationship. A wise man once said that we should always preach the Gospel, and, when necessary, use words. As we have seen in Jessica's case, caring relationships were more impactful than the specific words. We do not need to be perfect in our words. We need to be perfect in the way we love. As we join in God's work of helping others, Jeremiah offers us insight into what God will do for us. *I will refresh the weary and satisfy the faint. (Jer. 31:25)* This is hard work you are undertaking and yet the rewards are great, not only for the person you are journeying beside but also for you. *Peace I leave with you; my peace I give you. I do not give to you as the world gives. Do not let your hearts be troubled and do not be afraid. (John 14:27)*

If you could meet and talk with Maggie, Fred, or Pastor Nelson you might be surprised at how scared they were at the beginning of Jessica's crisis. They all expressed their feelings of being too unskilled to help. Yet help they did. All three would tell you that the only reason that they got through the stress without making too many mistakes is because they could each feel the presence of God's Holy Spirit guiding them. All three expressed that they had made many statements that they didn't know were important or helpful to Jess which were extremely critical at the time to her continuing search for mental health. Fred said it best when he said, "Many times I didn't know what to say but I'd open my mouth and out would come a most beautiful statement that I knew was not my wording." God has promised, *Because of the Lord's great love we are not consumed, for his compassions never fail. (Lam. 3:22)* If you give yourself to God's will then it is reasonable to trust that God will also grant you the best words to comfort and affirm. And when your day is through God will give you rest. *My presence will go with you, and I will give you rest. (Exod. 33:14)*

If you are excited about trying to help others, a word of caution is needed.

1. Establish or reinforce your relationship with the victim.

2. Go slowly. Uncovering trauma memories too quickly can lead to more trauma or even disintegration (Downing, 1993).

3. Be present to the person and try to connect him/her with a trained mental health professional.

4. Know your limits. Too many friends and family try to act like therapist but have little if any training. There is much to do even if you have no training in this area.

5. If the person rejects your help or rejects the idea of connecting with a therapist be patient but tenacious. Maggie is a good example to follow.

Remember, you are a valuable contributor to your friend's, family member's, or spouse's recovery. Do not underestimate your input and do not overestimate your skills. If you are in a quandary about what to say or do, call a mental health counselor and ask. If you do not know many people in your community try to get to know some of the resources around you. Keep a list of people who are referred to by others you meet and build your own list as you become more acquainted with the helpers in your community.

Blessing and peace to you as you minister to others who have been sexually traumatized as children.

Bibliography

Briere, J. and Runte, M. (1991). "The long-term effects of sexual abuse: a review and synthesis." *New Directions for Mental Health Services*, 51, 5-13.

Cheston, S. E. (1991). *Making Therapeutic Referrals*. New York: Gardner Press.

Downing, R. (1993). "Therapeutic tasks before uncovering trauma memories." Speech to Bay Ridge Counseling Center 9/27/93, Lutherville, Md.

Lew, M. (1990). *Victims No Longer*. New York: Harper & Row.

Linehan, M. M. (1993). *Skills Training Manual for Treating Borderline Personality Disorder*. New York: Guilford Press.

Scripture. *The Good News Bible*. (1976). New York: American Press Bible Society.

Wicks, R. and Parsons, R. D. (1993). *Clinical Handbook of Pastoral Counseling*, Vol 2. Mahwah, N.J.: Paulist Press.

Suggested Readings

Butler, S. (1985). *Conspiracy of Silence*. San Francisco: Volcano Press.

Finkelhor, D. (1984). *Child Sexual Abuse*. New York: Free Press.

Flaherty, S. (1992). *Woman, Why Do You Weep?* Mahwah, N.J.: Paulist Press.

Gil, E. M. (1983). *Outgrowing the Pain: A Book for and about Adults Abused as Children*. Walnut Creek, Calif.: Launch Press.

Rencken, R. H. (1989). *Intervention Strategies for Sexual Abuse*. Alexandria, Va.: AACD.

Rush, F. (1980). *The Best Kept Secret*. Englewood Cliffs, N.J.: Prentice-Hall.

Russell, D.E. (1986). *The Secret Trauma*. New York: Basic Books.

Other Books in the Series

Lessons from the Monastery that Touch Your Life
by M. Basil Pennington, O.C.S.O.

Little Pieces of Light...Darkness and Personal Growth
by Joyce Rupp

Spirituality, Stress & You
by Thomas E. Rodgerson